ABC & 123 COLORING BOOK

Belongs to

_____

_____

Test Your Color

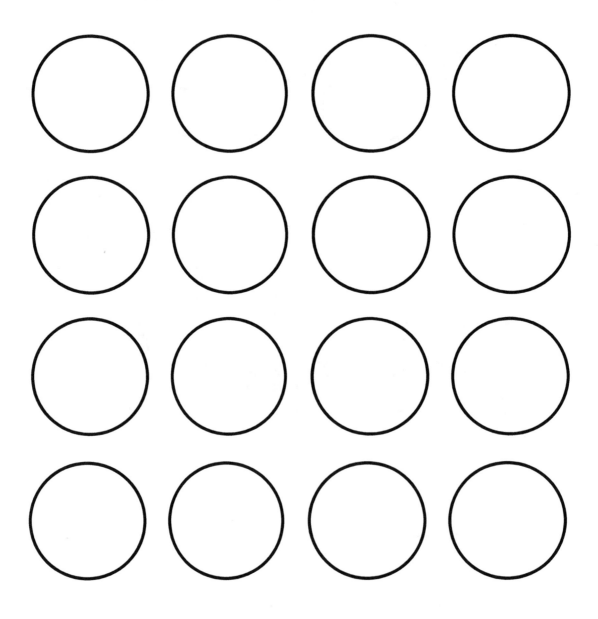

ABC & 123 COLORING BOOK

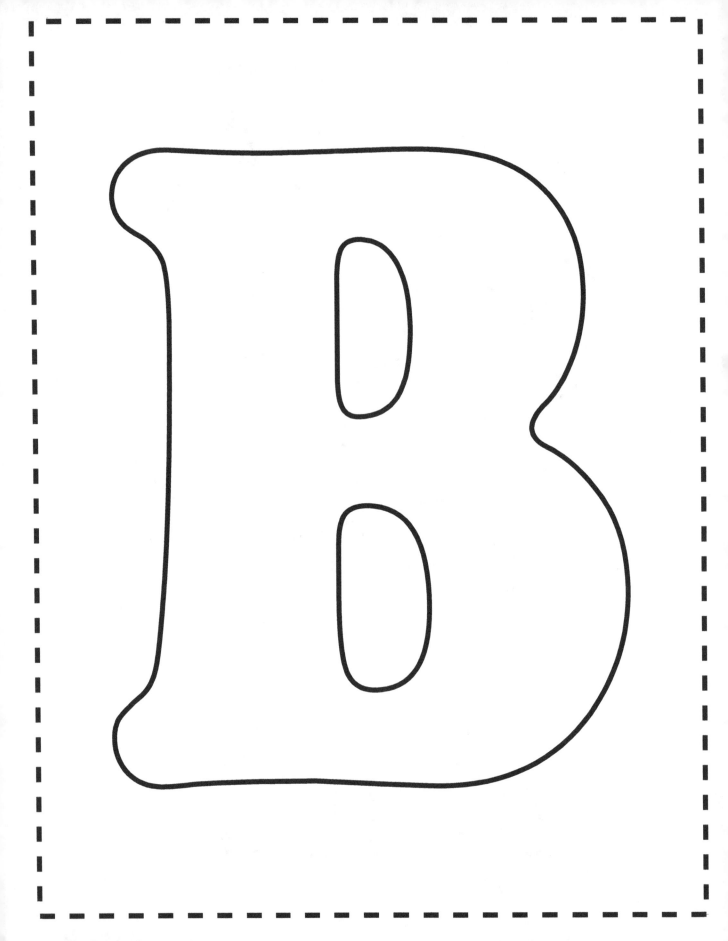

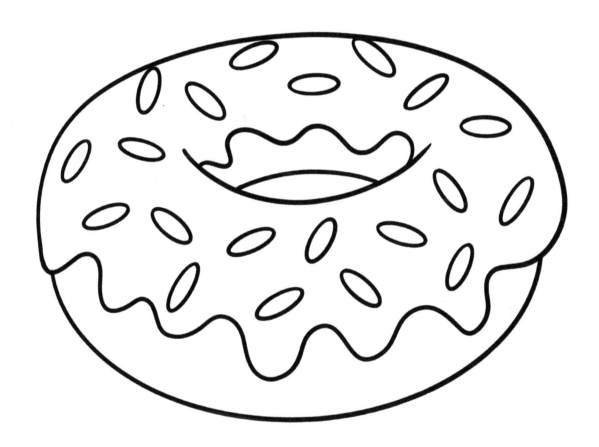

Donut

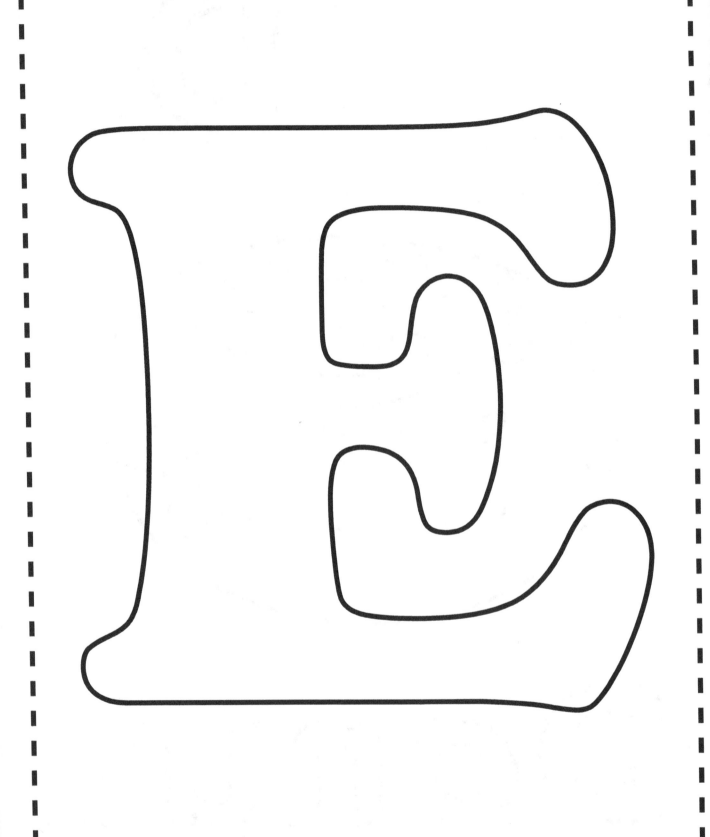

H

Hedgehog

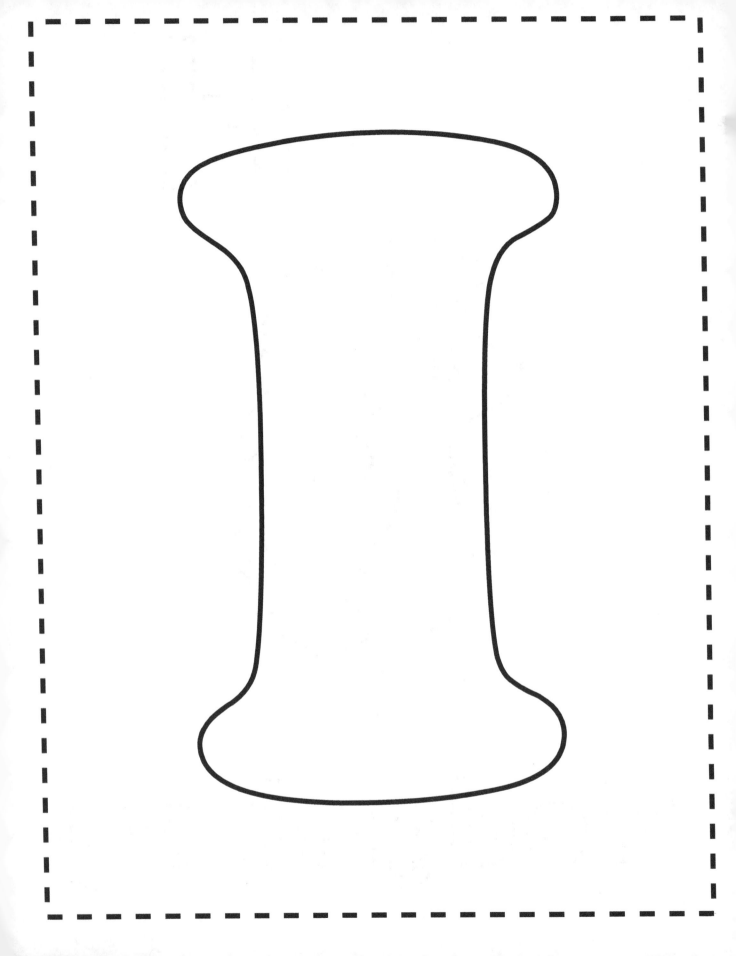

I

Ice cream

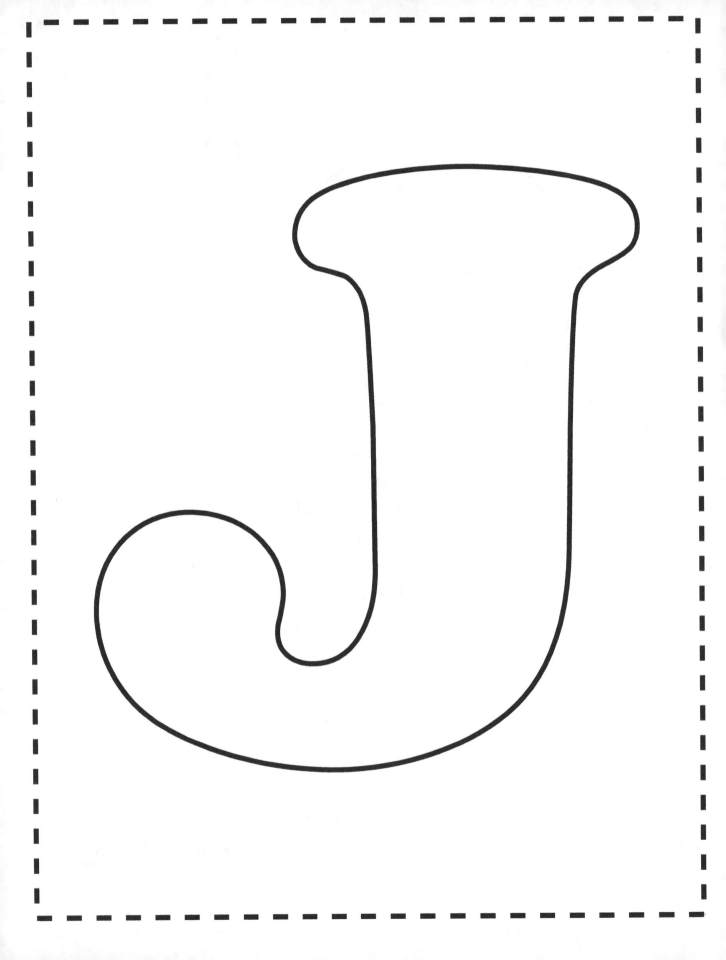

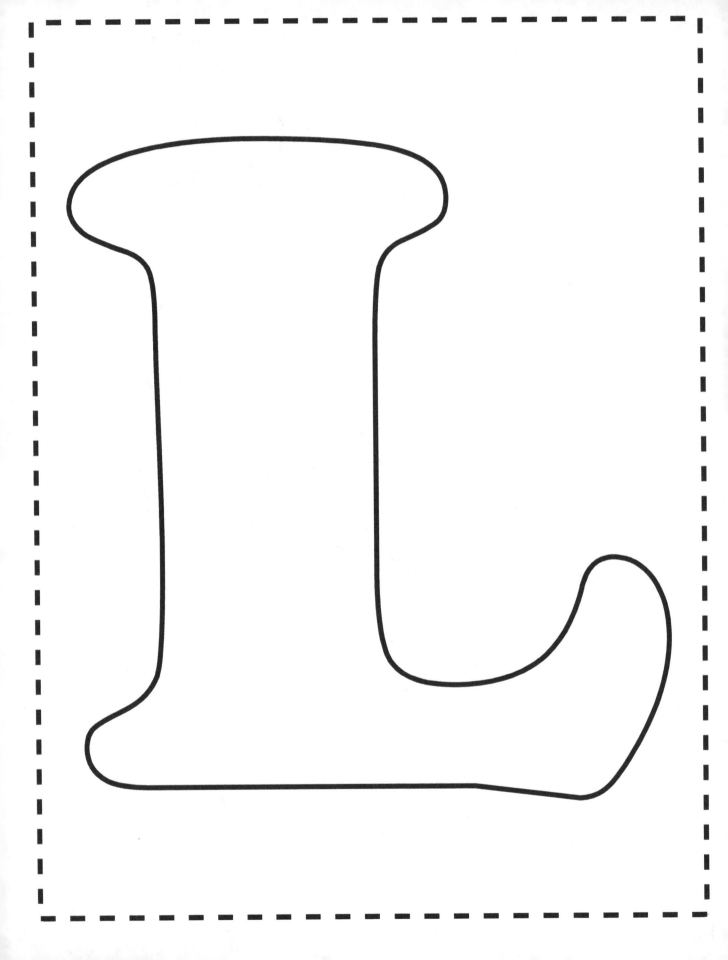

M

Mushroom

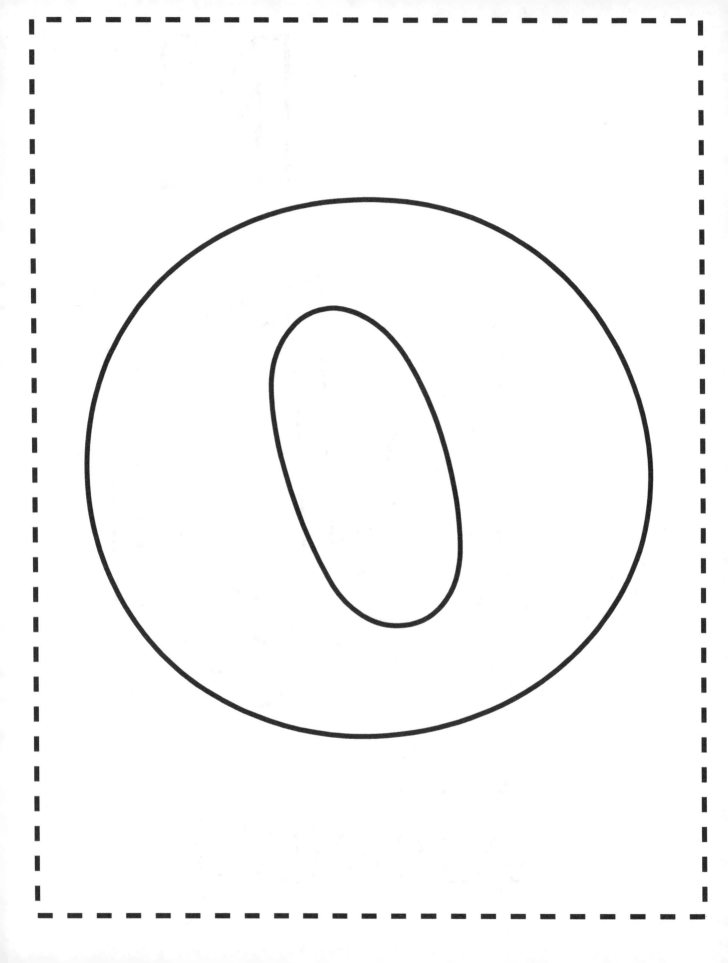

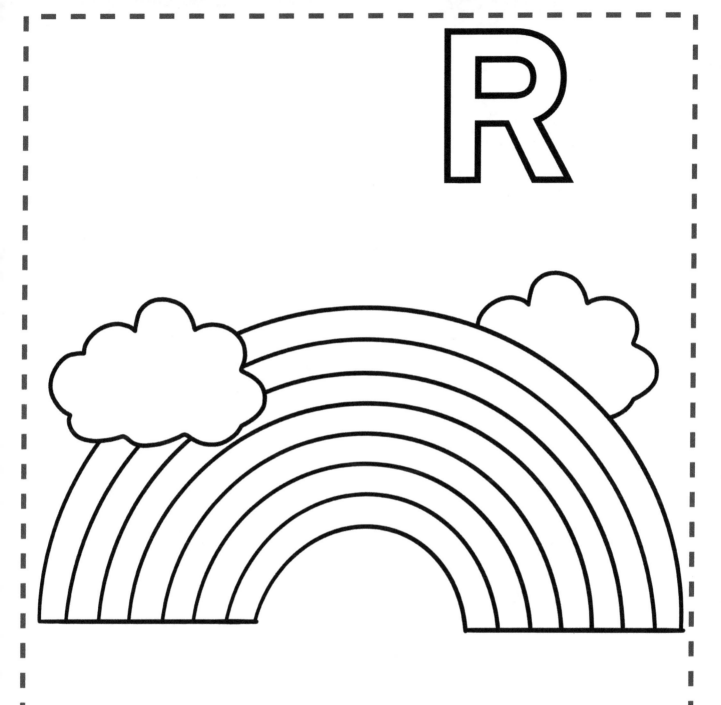

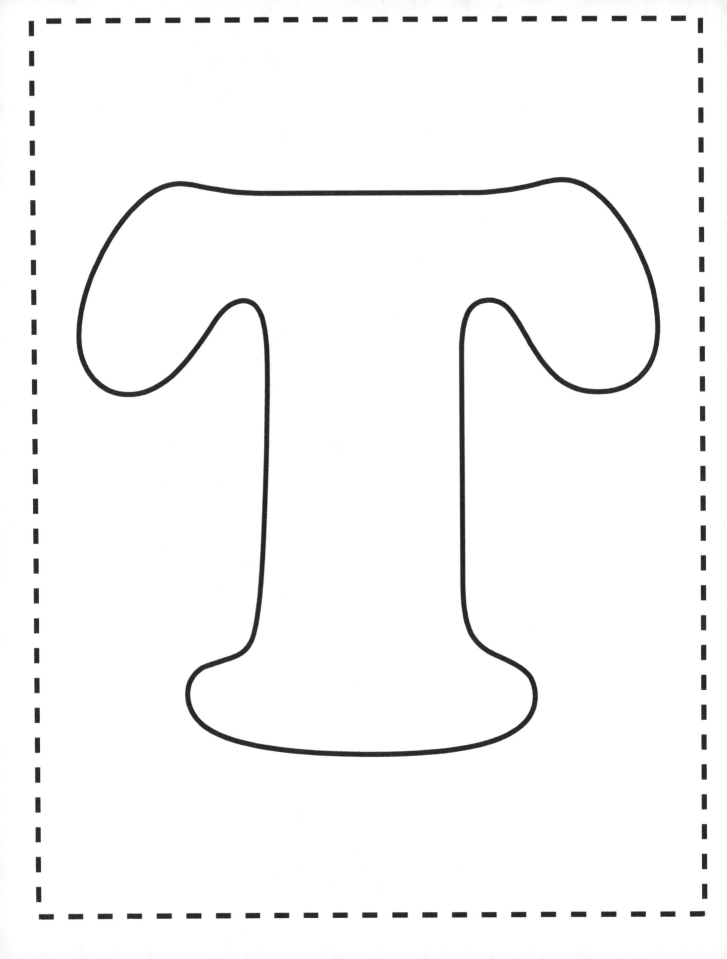

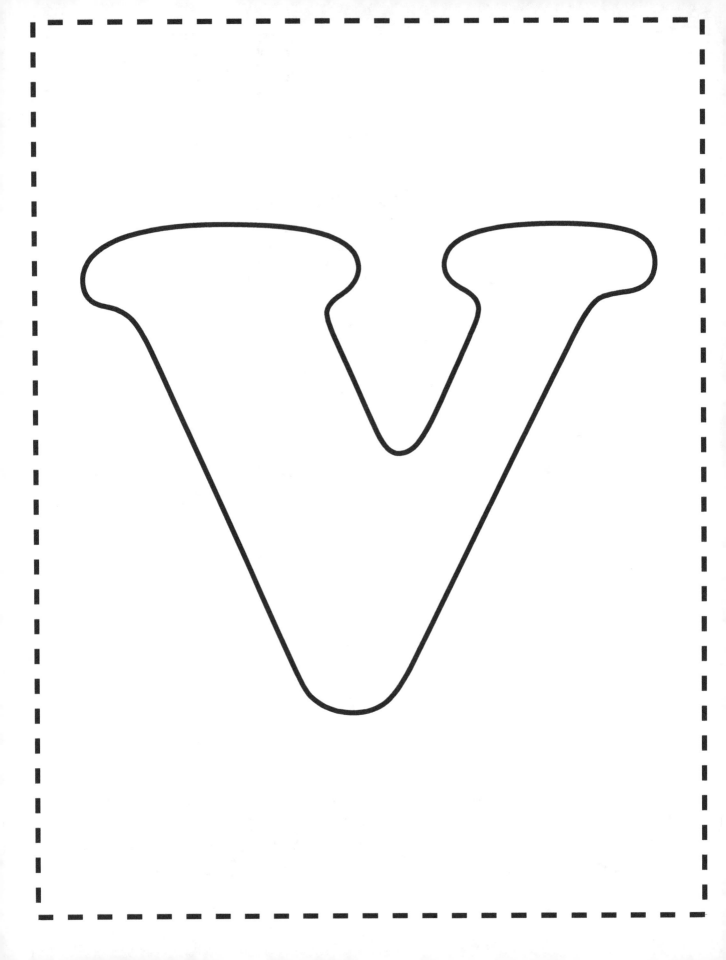

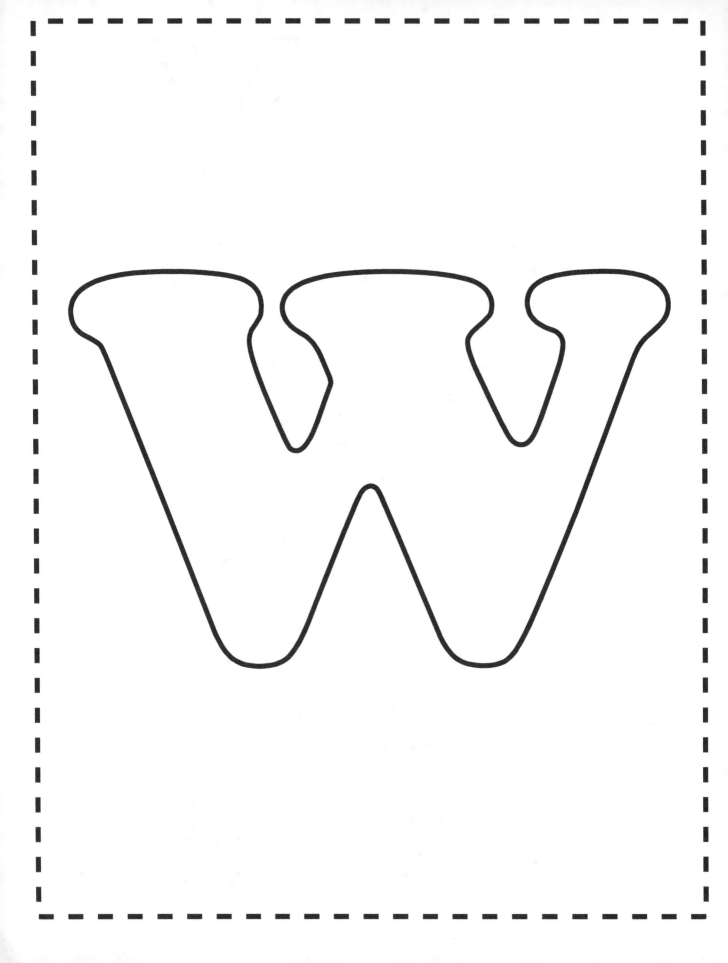

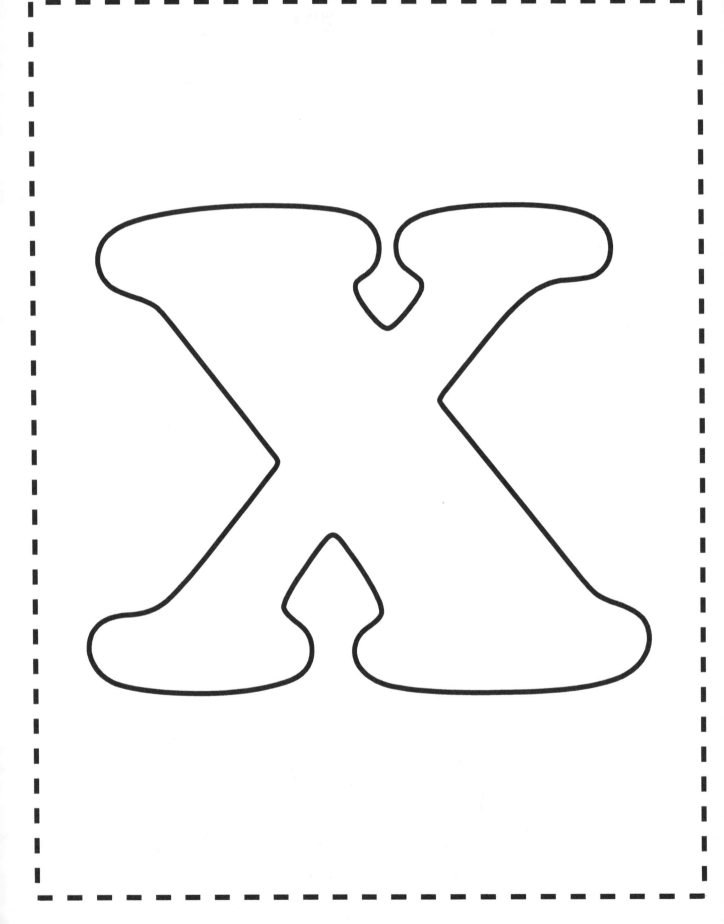

X-ray

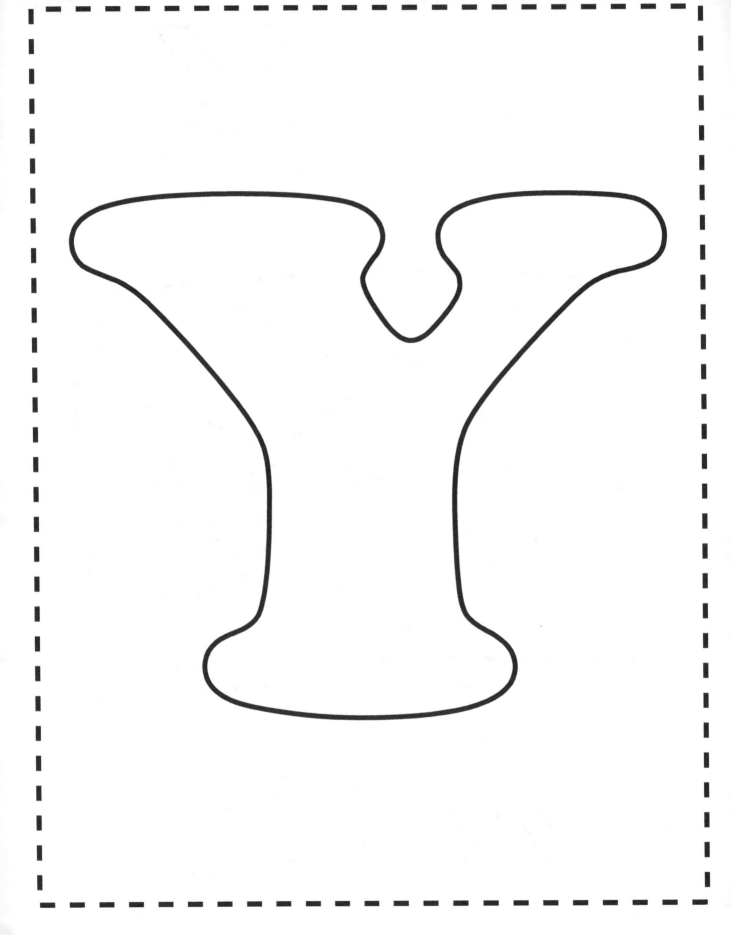

Test Your Color

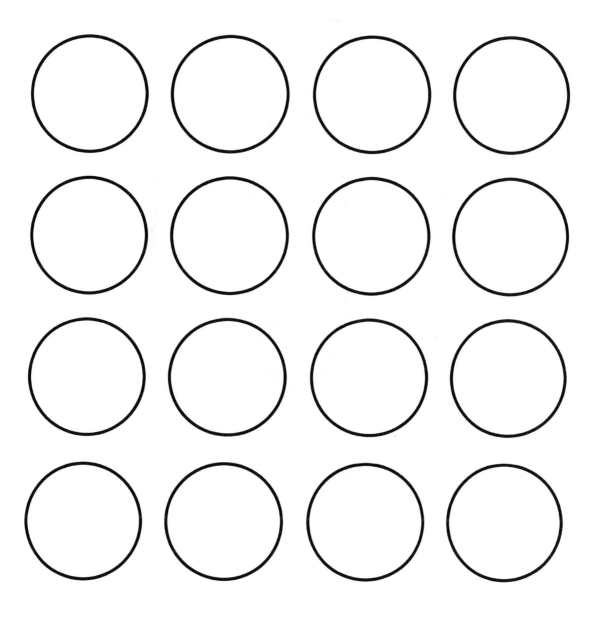

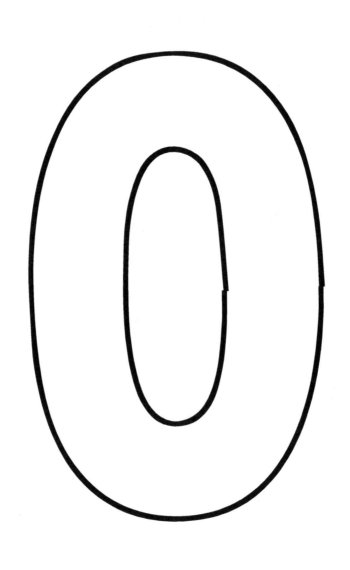

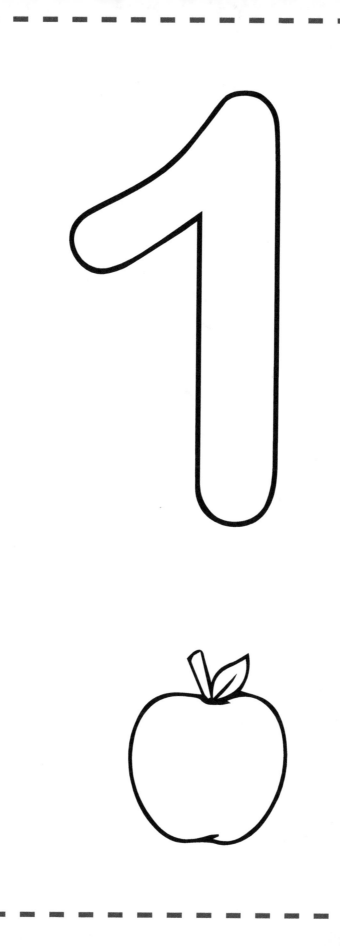

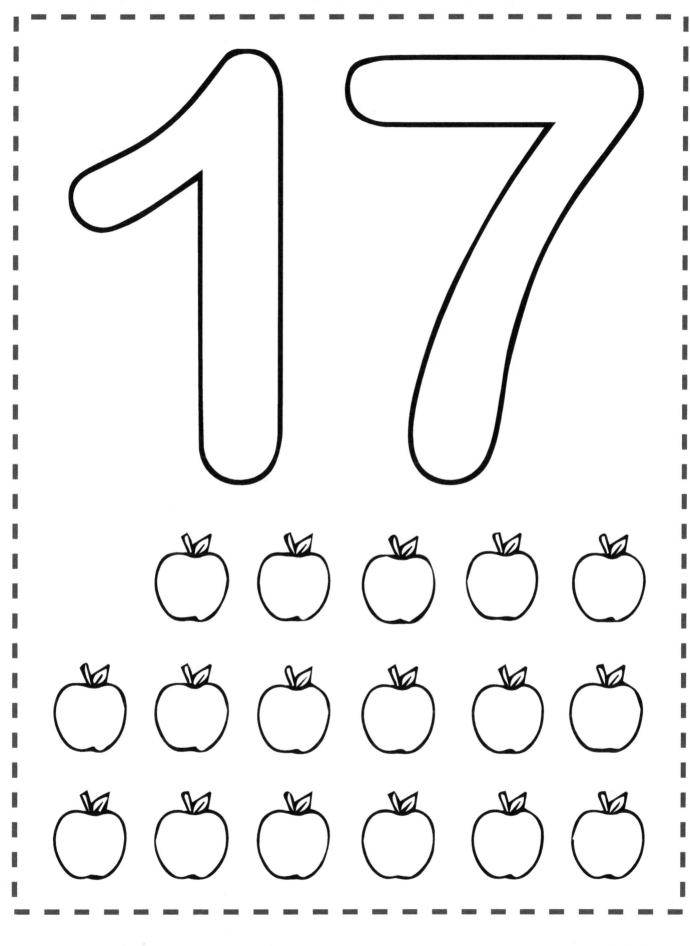

Kids

Activity

Fun

Count & Color

Fill numbers in the box.

3 + 🍬🍬🍬🍬 = ☐

1 + 🍬🍬🍬🍬🍬🍬 = ☐

4 + 🍭🍭🍭 = ☐

7 + 🍬🍬 = ☐

2 + 🍭🍭🍭🍭🍭 = ☐

Count & Color

Fill numbers in the box.

4 + 🐟 = ☐

6 + 🐻🐻 = ☐

2 + 🦆🦆🦆 = ☐

3 + 🐰🐰🐰🐰 = ☐

5 + 🦓🦓🦓 = ☐

Count & Color

Fill numbers in the box.

1 + 🫛🫛🫛🫛🫛🫛 = ☐

3 + 🥕🥕🥕🥕 = ☐

5 + 🥦🥦🥦 = ☐

2 + 🍅🍅🍅 = ☐

6 + 🍆🍆 = ☐

Count & Color

Fill numbers in the box.

8 + 🍎 = ☐

1 + 🍍🍍🍍🍍🍍🍍 = ☐

3 + 🍉🍉 = ☐

4 + 🍐🍐🍐🍐🍐 = ☐

5 + 🍓🍓🍓 = ☐

Count & Color

Fill numbers in the box.

4 + 🐘🐘🐘🐘 = ☐

6 + 🦉 = ☐

7 + 🐦🐦 = ☐

2 + 🦘🦘🦘 = ☐

1 + 🦛🦛 = ☐

Count & Color

Fill numbers in the box.

8 + 🦄 =

1 + 🦄🦄🦄🦄 =

3 + 🦄🦄🦄 =

5 + 🦄🦄 =

4 + 🦄🦄🦄 =

Count & Color

Fill numbers in the box.

Count & Color

Fill numbers in the box.

2 + 🚐🚐 = ☐

1 + 🛵🛵🛵 = ☐

6 + 🚗🚗 = ☐

8 + 🚌 = ☐

4 + 🛴 = ☐

Count & Color

Fill numbers in the box.

Count & Color

Fill numbers in the box.

7 + 🪐🪐 = ☐

6 + 🚀 = ☐

1 + ⭐⭐⭐⭐ = ☐

4 + 🪐🪐🪐 = ☐

3 + 🔭🔭 = ☐

How many children?

Color the picture & Count

Color the numbers that match the number of children in the picture.

2   4   3

How many dogs?

Color the picture & Count

Color the numbers that match the number of dogs in the picture.

2　　4　　3

How many cats?

Color the picture & Count

Color the numbers that match the number of cats in the picture.

How many shirts?

Color the picture & Count

Color the numbers that match the number of shirts in the picture.

How much fruit?

Color the picture & Count

Color the numbers that match the number of fruit in the picture.

How many cakes?

Color the picture & Count

Color the numbers that match the number of cakes in the picture.

5   2   3

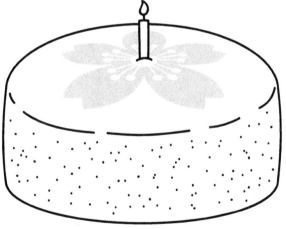

How many hats?

Color the picture & Count

Color the numbers that match the number of hats in the picture.

How many books?

Color the picture & Count

Color the numbers that match the number of books in the picture.

4　　　　　5　　　　　6

How many vegetables?

Color the picture & Count

Color the numbers that match the number of vegetables in the picture.

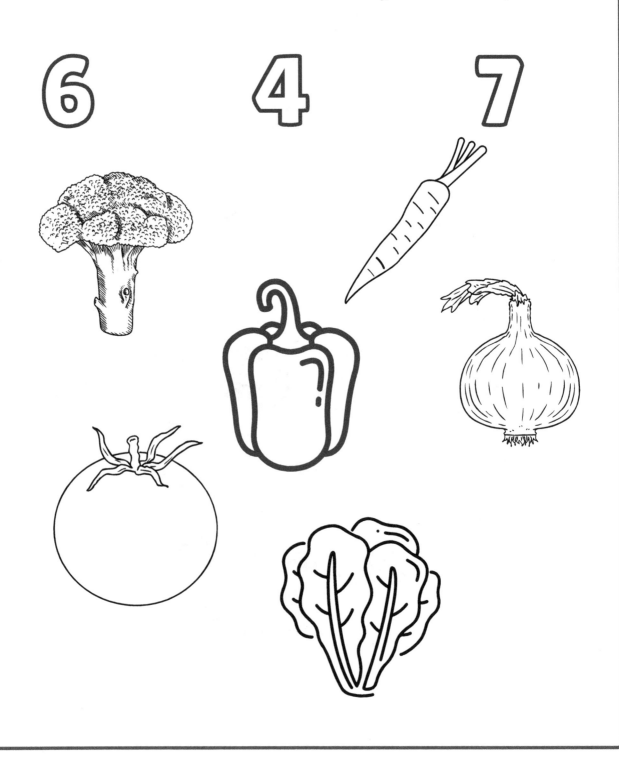

How many unicorns?

Color the picture & Count

Color the numbers that match the number of unicorns in the picture.

3 4 2

Draw anything

CPSIA information can be obtained
at www.ICGtesting.com
Printed in the USA
LVHW020816040623
748788LV00004B/102